THE CHRISTIAN CREEDS

A Faith To Live By

by Monika Hellwig

By the same author:
What Are the Theologians Saying?
The Meaning of the Sacraments

Foreword by Rev. Alfred M. McBride, O. Praem.

Pflaum/Standard
Dayton, Ohio

90057/6.8M/S8M-2-1073
Design: Tim Potter
Production: Linda Matthews

DEDICATION

For my sister, Angelika Collis,
and her children, Imogen, Oliver,
and Julia Claire

CONTENTS

THE CHRISTIAN CREEDS

A Faith To Live By

FOREWORD

Monika Hellwig writes with the conviction that theological talk should make a difference in people's lives. I heartily agree with her approach and admire the skill she employs in fulfilling her purpose. In this work on the Christian creeds she breathes considerable life into these household words of belief and worship.

I was particularly drawn to three tools that Dr. Hellwig used to let some primal light shine through the credal texts. First, her careful linkage of the material with the biblical mentality. In this she demonstrates that the creeds are far from being simply abstract religious statements, but rather declarations about the continual interaction between God and the Christian people. Just as the biblical datum was an announcement rising up from the jubilant meeting between humans and God, so also the creeds stand as further testimony that such religious experiences continued to occur.

Secondly, she locates the creeds in their historical context so that we can appreciate the special concerns and vocabulary of the various creed makers. The text without the context is a lifeless body; Dr. Hellwig makes sure we gain entry into the living situation.

Thirdly, she carefully shows how the creeds are grounded in and are grounds for a joyous hope. They are an antidote to what I would call the "problem psychosis" that sometimes grips people today. This psychosis is a symptom of those who decide that the current calamities of our time are the prelude to doomsday. Since, they claim, a dismal end awaits us all, the best we can do is cooperate in the collapse and operate in a horizon of despair. Monika Hellwig presents the creeds as signs of the coming of the victorious Lord, as forecasts of a New Jerusalem beyond the contemporary apocalypse, as a spur to our creative energies to solve our dilemmas, not to be overwhelmed by them.

I believe Dr. Hellwig has made an important statement here about our credal heritage, and I hope that multitudes will have the privilege of sharing her insights.

Rev. Alfred McBride, O.Praem.

INTRODUCTION: WHY THIS BOOK?

Like my two earlier books, *The Christian Creeds* is written for adult Christian believers, primarily Catholics, in search of a clearer understanding of their traditional faith in the modern world. I have written it because I am convinced that the task of the Christian theologian is first and foremost to be of service to the community of believers in its efforts to realize the vision of Jesus Christ. Whatever time theologians spend talking to one another in a language not understood outside their trade union has value only as preparation for their talking practical language to practical people. Practical language, of course, is not to be equated with non-religious or even with non-theological language. It is simply language that makes a difference to what people do in their lives and in their world.

When my first book was published some years ago, many readers responded, "This may be what the theologians are *saying*, but what the hell do they think they are *doing*? And why should we listen to what theologians say when we have the teachings of the Church?" My favorite Catholic Bishop said, "It's nice that you've written a book about what the theologians are saying, but don't you think we should begin to be more concerned about what the Church is saying?" So I took time out to write a book about the sacraments and teach a few more years, while thinking about the answer to these very significant questions.

A plain fact of history is that the theologian has always been somewhat perilously situated within the Church, and that people have been wondering for twenty centuries just what it is exactly that theologians were doing and what authority they had for doing it. A possibly more obscure fact of history is that what theologians thought they were doing at different times and places and in different types of theological investigation was not always completely explicit and was certainly not always the same. It is probably true to say that in the early ages of the Church it was primarily a matter of meditating on the Scriptures and gathering up the testimonies of earlier generations of Christians, and occasionally a matter of responding to philosophical questions and thinking out what ought to be Christian answers to questions arising from new cultural situations. This is certainly the impression one receives today reading collections of writings from the Patristic Era.

In the Middle Ages theology evolved into a systematic, rational or philosophical attempt to present a coherent view of Christian beliefs and their implications. In modern times a historical perspective came into the picture and everything became more complicated. In relation to the ancient creeds around which our statements of Christian belief have traditionally clustered, a new fact came to light. The Apostles' Creed, for instance, was not a text put together by the Apostles from the teachings of Jesus and carefully preserved ever since, as had been assumed without too much question for about a thousand years. It had grown out of the efforts of the community of believers to explain to newcomers, and to reduce to a short formula, what it was that Christians believed.

In the light of this information, one can no longer treat the Apostles' Creed as a timeless formula of faith, divinely given without having been influenced by cultural factors. Moreover, when we in the West began to hear the testimony of the Churches of the East again and to realize that they had been using not this Creed but several equally ancient and varying formulations, we had to admit something else. Evidently, there was not one uniform explanation of the faith at the beginning from which some groups broke away and made their own deviant formulations. There appears instead to have been a great deal of spontaneity and variety of improvisations in the earliest explanations and confessions of faith, and a tendency to freeze them gradually into certain agreed and official formulations. Once we know this from history, the question then arises as to what it was that unified the early Christian communities if the words explaining their faith varied and were only agreed upon gradually. Evidently what unified them was not so much to be found in words as in their way of life in the community in which they presently were, the experiences that community had shared in the past, and the hope that community had for the future. Whatever words they used to explain their faith made sense to them because of the life of the community which they shared and from which they knew the meaning of these short and rather mysterious statements.

In the early ages of the Christian era, the past experiences of the community and its future hope were fresh. The creeds came to be formulated from the way people expressed their experience and their hope. They had to be explained to newcomers, but the explanation was mainly by biblical stories and commentary upon them, by letting the newcomer share the prayer of the community and its life and memories. For various reasons, that freshness and practical personal involvement wore off with time. We know now that, even in the way churches were built and the Eucharist celebrated, the people moved farther and farther away from the altar and from an understanding of the language used. They also moved farther and farther away from the kind of experience and style of thinking in

9

which the great creeds of the churches were formulated. In the Middle Ages and on toward modern times, the wording of the creeds, like the shape of the liturgy and the various more elaborate definitions of doctrine, looked quite static, as though they had been given in that form in the very beginning by Jesus to the Apostles. The role of the Holy Spirit in the Church was perhaps not fully understood.

This is why the creeds and definitions of doctrine, that is, the teachings of the Church, need to be explained. This is why the explanation is not simple, nor easy. The theologian does not deal with a list of vocabulary items that have quite clear definitions on which there has always been agreement. He does not deal with a sequence of Church pronouncements, all of which are in agreement. He really deals with twenty centuries of combined and sometimes stormy efforts to give expression to an experience and a hope that are in themselves inexpressible. He deals with testimony of twenty centuries in which people used different languages and used them in very different ways according to their very different cultural experiences.

The theologian has to do more than teach theology. He makes theology. And theologians of each generation still have to make theology. They cannot simply pass on what was done in another age, because the work of redemption is still going on. We still have to try to listen to what the Spirit is saying in and to the Church as history unfolds and new generations of men take part in shaping the future. We have to ask constantly whether this shaping of the future is helping or hindering the hope of Christians. When we ask that question in relation to one practical question such as that of conscientious objection to a war, or cultivation of human life in a test tube, we often find that we also have to ask the most basic questions again, such as what we mean by redemption or salvation, what it really is that Christians hope, what it is that the doctrine of creation tells us about the human situation in the world.

The fact that we cannot at once answer the particular practical question shows that there is a gap between our real experience of life and the decisions we have to make, and our profession of faith in Jesus Christ as the key to what we think are the goal and meaning of life. We can deal with that gap in two ways. We can assume that it is meant to be there and that the Christian message of redemption is concerned not with the everyday substance of human experience and action but with something more ethereal and remote. In other words, we can assume that Jesus Christ brings a message that is not meant to make a real difference in the world or in what people do to shape the history of mankind in the world, that his message only summons people to a response of faith and trust in the secret depths of their hearts which they express in prayer and churchly activities and for which they are rewarded after death, but which leaves the world, and what goes on in the world, unchanged. One might even conclude that the world cannot be redeemed, that, at most, individual souls of men can be redeemed out of the world.

Catholic thought and teaching has characteristically rejected this way of dealing with the gap between experience and the confession of faith. Modern Scripture scholarship confirms this Catholic insistence by showing that it would be very difficult to interpret the teaching of Jesus about the Kingdom of Heaven in this way in the light of what we know of the existing notion of the Kingdom of God in Israel at the time of Jesus.

One would have to distort the evidence quite a bit to do it, as will be explained in Chapter II, "What Christians Hope For."

The alternate way of dealing with the gap between experience and the confession of faith is to assume that it is not meant to be there and to ask how it came about, and how it can be bridged again. That can only be done with great respect for tradition, for the primacy of the Spirit in the living of the Christian way of life, for the wisdom that comes from the living out of the Christian commitment in practice rather than the kind of knowledge that is merely speculative. Whenever theologians ask the basic questions about the meaning of redemption, of Christian hope, of creation, of Christ, in order to make a new attempt to solve new practical questions, they find that in fact they are doing several very different kinds of work.

The most fundamental level of work in theology, on which everything else rests, is pure research or information retrieval. It is concerned with finding out simply what was in fact done, said, written, organized and thought, by whom, when, where. Because everything else rests on this foundation, theologians very often find they must retrace the steps by which earlier generations came to their explanations of the meaning of doctrines. They must challenge or question some conclusions that have long been unquestioned, simply because new facts have come to light.

A second level is the task of interpreting the meaning of statements and actions, by looking at the context in which they happened, what is known about the understanding and questions and experience of the people who spoke or acted. In our day, cultural anthropology, the study of people in different cultures and their different ways of life, has made us more alert to the fact that even simple words like "brother" or "father" and simple actions, like breaking a loaf of bread or touching someone on the shoulder, have different meanings in different societies. Therefore we know that, to understand what was meant in the apostolic and patristic writings by key phrases and actions, we have to learn the cultural background as thoroughly as possible with our present methods of information retrieval and try to interpret what those words and deeds meant to their authors. At this level it is always partly guesswork, but theologians try to do the guesswork honestly and intelligently, weighing all the known information and allowing for all the gaps. Further levels in theology again rest upon this, and the conclusions and explanations are called in question whenever a reconstruction of the meaning at this level has to be modified or replaced by a more probable one.

A third level of work in theology is the very difficult one of putting such reconstructions together into a historical sequence, in order to try to see the line of development, to understand how various formulations and conclusions and viewpoints were reached, to try to see how they reflected the experience of the Christian communities that reached them. This is quite complicated because it involves not only, for instance, what Augustine thought about a question of grace or the Trinity and what Aquinas thought about it and what the Fathers at the Council of Trent thought about it. It also involves what Aquinas thought Augustine thought, and what the Fathers of Trent thought Aquinas thought, and what they thought he thought Augustine thought Scripture meant on these points. Again, it is obviously a matter for reconstruction by intelligent, intellectually honest and humble guesswork, and in the course of time the reconstructions have to be criticized and modified.

The real purpose of these steps is to have some grounds for the fourth level, that of trying to discern the clearest, most accurate interpretation of the Christian message. That does not mean that there cannot be alternate explanations, different ways of expressing fundamental doctrines of the tradition. But it does mean that, in order to live by the Christian gospel, one very often must make a choice between opposing interpretations, where both cannot be right if the gospel is to make sense at all. In such choices the questions cannot always be resolved by sheer scholarship. There is already a polemic built into the question.

At this level the teaching authority of the Church has always been seen as an essential partner in the discussion by Catholic theologians. Judging by logic and speculative reasoning alone, one might arrive at a comprehensive viewpoint from several different perspectives which would lead to very different styles of life and action. But if the practical experience of Christian living is to be a deciding factor, the theologian is not any more expert in this by virtue of his occupation than other sincere Christians. It becomes a matter for discernment as to where, among contradictory viewpoints, the Spirit is breathing in the Church. In the struggle of the believing community to see this, Catholic tradition places the authoritative expression of that discernment in the competence of the hierarchic authority of the Church. It is not an academic but a practical competence that is at stake here.

If Catholics were to expect, as they have sometimes, that questions at the earlier three levels would be resolved by the authoritative voice of the hierarchy of the Church, they would be disappointed. They would, in fact, be confusing two different kinds of authority or competence—the authority to command and be obeyed because of an office of leadership or government in the community, and the authority of expertise or knowing the matter thoroughly, which is an authority to explain and be believed. When it is a matter of information retrieval, ascertaining the meaning that words or actions had when first used, and reconstructing lines of historical development, it is the authority of expertise that is helpful.

The reason for the hierarchic authority at the fourth level as an important factor is that there is another whole phase, another whole side to theology that has not been mentioned yet. This is the phase that begins with an integrated Christian commitment, elaborates the doctrines or beliefs that express this commitment, explores and explains their contemporary meaning in a complete and integrated way, and communicates the explanation to those concerned to know it. This whole phase obviously depends very much on its practitioners' really having made a personal commitment of faith in Jesus Christ in the context of his Church, while the first phase, the four levels mentioned, depends more exclusively simply on competent and painstaking scholarship.

If some Catholics, including many members of the hierarchy, are not much at ease with what theologians are doing today, it is partly because what they are doing is complex and has many levels and stages, but it is also surely because so much effort is concentrated on the first phase and relatively little is being done on the other side of theology today. As a result, bishops, pastors, preachers and catechists find they have access to lots of subtle and sophisticated questions and problems that they can pass along but somehow seem unable to lay hands on books that offer them a positive content giving a rounded account of Catholic faith today.

There are, in fact, theologians working in this spirit and producing an account of Catholic faith that can be communicated to those anxious to live it rather than merely sharpen their wits discussing it. But there still appears to be a rather large communication gap between the language and style of those who are doing this and the language and style in which it must be done in order to reach the people for whom it is ultimately intended. It is the purpose of this book, on the confession of faith that we make in our standard creeds, to try to bridge the gap, in one respect at least.

NOTES

The account here of the various levels and aspects of the work of theologians is more or less that of Bernard Lonergan in the second chapter of his book, *Method in Theology* (Herder and Herder, 1971).

Two books available in English that give the type of integrated presentation spoken of in the last paragraph of this introduction are *Introduction to Christianity* by Josef Ratzinger (Herder and Herder, 1970) and *The Christ* by Piet Schoonenberg (Herder and Herder, 1971). Both are fairly heavy reading and use language less familiar to non-theologians, and both are focused on specialized areas of Christian doctrine. Coming much closer to the expectations of the ordinary inquiring Catholic is *God Our Savior* by Peter de Rosa (Bruce, 1967). This last book sets out to answer the questions of what we really mean by salvation and in what sense we need to be saved. In the course of answering these questions, it gives a rounded account of the content of Christian faith.

CHAPTER I — WHAT IS A CREED?

To this question most Catholics would answer that it is a summary of what Christians believe. Some would say it is a kind of prayer recited at the Sunday celebration of the Eucharist and at baptisms and other occasions. Some might think of it as a kind of loyalty oath. In fact, it is all of these things, but some explanation may be helpful.

At the Sunday Mass we recite a Creed usually referred to as the Nicene Creed. This is historically inaccurate, but not, for practical purposes, a problem. At the Council of Nicaea in 325 A.D., the Council Fathers discussed the adoption of a creed already customary at Caesarea and decided that it did not solve the particular questions they had about the relation of Jesus to the Father. They put together a more elaborate one which included a section at the end condemning those who would maintain any one of a list of statements contradicting the creed they had agreed upon. But this is not the Creed that we recite at Mass. At the Council of Constantinople in 381 A.D., a very similar creed was approved, adding quite a lengthy section concerning the Christian understanding of the Spirit and the Church, but dropping the "anathemas," that is, the condemnations of people who maintain otherwise. This was solemnly read and approved at the Council of Chalcedon in 451 A.D. and has become a central creed in Christian liturgical worship under the name of Nicene Creed.

One very interesting factor of this history is the dropping of the "anathemas." The creeds used in worship are primarily a short form of profession of faith of the worshipping community; as such, they are not only a summary of the content of faith but also a prayer in which the believing community renews its commitment. In that context there is really no place for condemnation of opposing forces. Although it does indeed function as a loyalty oath, this is quite adequately expressed in a positive formulation.

Another interesting factor in the history is the pattern of adding and dropping, piecing together, rewording, comparing creeds of different local churches and devising words and phrases to cope with new questions or problems. Evidently, in the first few centuries Christians tolerated a good deal of ambiguity in the words used. As already mentioned in the introduction to this book, their unity seems to have rested basically on their shared way of life and their shared prayer and meditation on Scripture. They did not begin from agreement on a formulation of beliefs. They seemed to work toward that from time to time as particular problems arose, and those problems normally had something to do with judgments as to how to live a Christian life.

This gives a clue to what a Creed really is. It is not an exhaustive statement, even in summary, of the Christian worldview. It is most certainly not a philosophical interpretation of reality, or of history, or of human existence. It is first and foremost a statement of the grounds for Christian hope. It does not really spell out that hope but assumes it. It does not state everything that Christians believe, but only those grounds of hope that have seemed particularly important for the community to confess or that have been questioned, thereby challenging the unity of the Church of believers in Jesus Christ.

This means that very important aspects of Christian life and faith are not mentioned. The ancient creeds that we recite in worship, mainly the "Nicene" and the Apostles' Creeds, do not for instance mention the Eucharist, while the Creed of the Council of Trent, promulgated in 1564 (which we do not use in worship), specifies seven sacraments and an elaborate theology of the Eucharist.

Although the ancient creeds have been used for worship, they were originally devised not for a renewal of commitment at the beginning of the Sunday Eucharist, but as a solemn formula of profession of faith by an adult candidate for baptism at the end of his course of catechetical instructions. From there, they seem to have found their way into the ceremony of baptism itself. The forms we now have represent a consensus that emerged only in the course of time from many local traditional creeds, embodying what the local churches thought was essential for a newcomer to accept and understand in order to preserve the faith handed down from the Apostles.

That faith, however, has been expressed in many confessions (statements of belief), formal and informal, liturgical and personal, simple and complex, that never became official creeds. The simple believer, the theologian, and the hierarchic authority in the Church all have to take these into account and put them together to give a full and rounded account of what Christians believe and have believed from the beginning.

The earliest testimony that we have suggests that at the core of the Christian message is the conviction that "God has made both Lord and Christ this Jesus whom you crucified" (Acts 2:36). Although this statement sounds simple enough, it has an enormous amount of meaning packed into it and is the heart of all subsequent creeds. It affirms belief in Jesus as divine savior and relates this saving role to his having been executed as a criminal. It is worded simply as a statement of fact in the past tense, but when one re-

21

fiects on what is stated it is quite clear that more than an intellectual assent or dissent to the truth of the statement is called for.

We have grown so accustomed to the expression, Jesus Christ, that many people think of Christ simply as a surname, which is an ordinary proper name. But Christ or Messiah means the one who ushers in the Reign of God, that is, that final time in which suffering and sin and death are to be overcome. In other words, he is the one who is the answer to all the troubles of mankind, the one who holds the key to the ultimate solution of all the problems of history. But the Apostles' testimony goes further than that by saying that God has made Jesus both Lord and Christ. They tell us that Jesus stands in an absolutely unique relationship to God whom the Jews called Father and whom Jesus addressed by an intimate family pet name for Father. They tell us that the Apostles recognized Jesus as the Son of God, that in him they actually met God and that this opened their eyes so that they crossed over into a new life. But they link this to his having been executed as a criminal. They tell everybody that on the third day after his death, God raised him up from the dead, that they, the Apostles, are witnesses of it and that in this experience they recognized who he really was and their lives were changed.

We are so accustomed to thinking of Jesus as divine savior that it is easy to miss the strange contradiction and challenge in the message the Apostles preached. Listening to it now, many Christians see it as a churchly message about an otherworldly salvation that happens after death and which is well guaranteed by a great church structure and a long church history. When it was first proclaimed it was anything but churchly, because the religious authorities were pre-

cisely the ones who said that Jesus could not sub-
stantiate his claims about the Reign of God. In fact,
they had concurred in his condemnation and execution.
Moreover, in its Jewish setting it was not really otherworldly, because the Jewish expectation of the Reign
of God was not really otherworldly, as will be explained in the next chapter. Neither was the message
backed by any very convincing guarantee. The Apostles
claimed to be witnesses of his Resurrection, but they
stated that the soldiers and other unbelievers had not
been such witnesses and admitted implicitly that none
of the enemies of Jesus had experienced his resurrection. In fact they said we all ought to believe them,
just because they had been witnesses and that their
changed lives were the evidence to us that they had
been such witnesses.

When looked at in its context, this is a strange and
far-reaching claim. People are being asked to call success what certainly looks like failure, to call life what
certainly looks like death, and to look for salvation and
hope in what seems to be destruction. To give any
kind of assent to the message the Apostles preached
means turning a great many values and assumptions
about life in this world upside down. We usually suppose that the laws and institutions of society help
men in living human lives, that properly constituted
authority is to be respected and trusted, and that when
people are executed as criminals it is because they are
enemies of society and a threat to other men. In other
words, we suppose that God's will for mankind is
somehow embodied by the authority and simply by
what, in fact, "works" in society. According to the basic
proclamation that Jesus who has been crucified is
both Lord and Christ, believers in the message of the
Apostles can really never take these assumptions for
granted again.

23

It may still be possible to miss the shock or scandal of the preaching of Christ crucified, by supposing that the Jews and the Romans at the time of Jesus were a quite peculiarly wicked combination of powerholders and nation builders, and that that made this particular situation so different and so tragic. But the evidence suggests rather that the particular colonial regime in power was in many respects rather enlightened and that many of the actors in the death of Jesus were more or less in good faith.

The more one comes to grips with what the Jews were really talking about when they spoke of expecting the Reign of God, and the more one tries to understand what the Apostles were saying in that context, the clearer it becomes that they had a very radical message, based on a whole new vision of life and the reality of God and man.

As long as the young Christian community was preaching to its Jewish neighbors, much could be taken for granted in the presentation of the Christian message or gospel. They could preach Jesus crucified as the Son of God, the revealing Word of God, the Messiah or anointed of God, the one raised from the dead by God to sit at his right hand. They could be sure the initial impact would be to shock and scandalize, but that at least their Jewish friends knew exactly what they meant by God, and agreed with them about man's relation to God by creation and vocation. In fact, it was precisely because their Jewish friends knew exactly what they meant by God that they were so shocked at the claims about Jesus.

When the community began to preach among gentiles, a new problem arose. It could by no means assume that the listeners shared the Christians' understanding of God. We get an indication of the nature of the problem in the Acts of the Apostles, chapter 17, when Paul is reported as preaching to philosophically inclined Greeks at the Areopagus in Athens. In a lengthy passage, verses 22-34, we are given an account of Paul's effort to explain to these people what he means by God and to link the question with Jesus and the resurrection. He is having considerable difficulty, and indeed, when he concludes, he is ridiculed. These philosophically inclined people are quite happy to discuss the existence and nature of God in the abstract as long as it does not connect with real events in history where they might be challenged to question and change the values and understanding by which they live their everyday lives. In other words, they do not object to philosophical discussion about God as long as it does not really make any difference in life.

As a matter of fact, this is not too different today. Many people at universities and elsewhere are happy to discuss God as an abstraction on which to sharpen their logic and epistemology, but when the discussion relates this God to concrete events in history that might make a difference, they are likely to ridicule this as irrelevant to "the question" and unsophisticated. This is precisely where the "scandal" of the Christian message arises.

Paul was having difficulty not only because the crowd did not want to hear the message he had to preach, but also because at the heart of the Christian message is the cross of Jesus and not any speculation about God. The earliest core of the message simply takes the God of Israel for granted. It is not unlikely that Paul and others in similar circumstances found that, because they had not had to explain before what they meant by God, because they had been raised in a society where everyone "knew" God, it was difficult to put their idea of God into words. They may not have had a clear idea of God in any conceptual sense. What they had was an experience of the Jewish community's response to God and a wealth of poetic stories about man's relation to God in the Hebrew scriptures.

Again, this is really not so different from the contemporary Christian. If an ordinary, good Christian, instructed in the catechism, fairly well read in the scriptures, attentive at sermons, were asked to explain what he meant by God, he would probably be puzzled, for exactly the same reason. At the heart of the message that has been handed on to him is Jesus Christ, divine savior, who really lived and suffered and died and on the third day rose from the dead to sit at God's right hand. But in the content of Christian faith as handed on to him there is very little speculation about God. *God is taken for granted.*

If one were to press the man in the street, or man in the pew, he would be likely eventually to recall that God is our Father, and that God created heaven and earth and everything in them, and that God "can do everything." This is what eventually found its way into the creeds, by way of explanation of what we mean by God. What is interesting is that it contains absolutely no speculation about what God essentially is; it addresses itself only to what God means to us. This is more or less deliberate. Ever since the time of Paul, we have realized that our essential message concerns Jesus, that is, Jesus crucified, and that whatever does not elucidate that message is hot air. Speculation about the nature of God is not particularly helpful to the believer because, first of all, we can never know anything more than what God is not, and because it is in no way our business to know what God "really" is, and because, if we did know this, it would not make a difference.

What the churches did in the course of time, when they added a section explaining what they meant by God at the beginning of the creeds, was to refer to the existing scriptures, tradition, and worship of Israel. They took key ideas from the biblical stories of the creation, the election of Israel and the vindication of the chosen people against their rivals who followed "other gods." Thus they describe God as maker of everything, Father, and all-powerful.

While the witnesses and preachers were still very close in time to the life of Jesus and the events following upon his death, they claimed the authority of eyewitnesses to the events as validation of their preaching. With distance from the events in time, and also in space and culture and language, the question had to be asked again how the authority for preaching was communicated. From earliest times an answer took shape which, in retrospect, we can call the typically Catholic answer. The authority is communicated in the Church, that is, in the community of the followers of Jesus, sharing their understanding of the gospel and sure that they will always have a true understanding because the Spirit of Jesus, which is the breath of God, is with them as Jesus promised.

How that Spirit may be recognized amid the confusion of many voices, and what makes up the Church, are very difficult questions even to our own times and will be discussed in Chapters 6 and 7. It was in response to questions of this kind that the third section of the creed about the Holy Spirit and the Church took shape. The Spirit and the Church, like God, could be taken for granted at the beginning.

These introductory observations on the coming to

be and the content of the creeds in their trinitarian shape ought to bring into focus one further point. When we say at the beginning of a creed, "I believe in" and at the end, "Amen," there is a distinctive meaning to the believing. One might casually assume that "I believe in God" is simply parallel to "I believe in flying saucers" or "I believe in the Loch Ness monster," meaning, "I have not seen any of these but I believe that they exist." This, however, is clearly not the meaning. It is more closely parallel to "I believe in you," meaning "I have not yet experienced what you are going to achieve but I am confident that you can and will do it." If I say, "I believe in you, in your good judgment, your courage, and your promise," I mean, in effect, that I have confidence in you because of your good judgment, your courage and your promise. This is closely akin to the meaning of "I believe" in the creed where we place our confidence and our hope in God who redeems us in his Son, Jesus, and whose Spirit is with us until the task of redemption is complete. When we say, "Amen," it is not parallel to an oath that what has just been said is the truth, the whole truth and nothing but the truth. It is parallel rather to someone saying "Count me in."

NOTES

Texts of the early creeds with brief introductions are available in *Documents of the Christian Church* selected & edited by Henry Bettenson (Oxford University Press, 1963).

An extensive discussion of the history of the creeds and the issues behind them is available in *Early Christian Creeds* by J.N.D. Kelly (Longmans, 1950). An interesting and more popularly written discussion of the meaning of the early creeds in their historical context, written by a Protestant New Testament scholar, is *From the Apostles' Faith to the Apostles' Creed* by O. Sydney Barr (Oxford University Press, 1964).

CHAPTER II—WHAT CHRISTIANS HOPE FOR

From earliest times Christian preaching was referred to as the "gospel," meaning good news. The gospel is not only or primarily good news about something that happened in the past, long ago. If it were just that, people could look at the sin and suffering in the world today—at war, and crime on the streets, and needless pain and poverty, and mass selfishness and greed—and they might comment that it is nice to know that something good happened twenty centuries ago, but that it is also rather irrelevant because it does not seem to have made any difference to the life we live today.

The good news is primarily concerned with a hope and a promise for the future, substantiated by an event that has already taken place. The core of the message concerns what there is to hope for, but from the beginning it was hidden in the claim that Jesus is the Christ. Only later does it come to be made a little more explicit in the creeds when we say that we wait for "the resurrection of the dead and the life of the world to come" in the Nicene Creed, and that we believe in "the resurrection of the body and life everlasting" in the Apostles' Creed.

The phrases are so familiar that often Catholics think they know what these words mean just because they have heard them so often since childhood. If a Catholic is asked what it is he hopes for, he will most likely answer, "Heaven." Asked what he means by heaven, he may hesitate longer, and describe it as the reward that God has in store for those who respond to his invitation by faith, hope and charity, which means leading a good life. Pressed what that reward is, he will most likely say that this is something no one can know until after he dies.

If this is followed by the question whether he does

not expect any reward during this life, the ordinary, good Catholic may find himself in a dilemma. On the one hand, his concept of heaven does clearly refer to a fulfillment of human hopes and aspirations in some wonderful and indescribable way beyond death. On the other hand, all of us harbor a wistful, sneaking hope that if men live good lives, oriented to God in faith and hope and charity, their lives ought to be happier because of this. We feel that any just and reasonable and all-powerful God must surely have things arranged so that if we do the right thing, things do indeed go right. Any other arrangement seems so absurd, so pointless, that it seems somehow less than worthy of a good God.

No matter what official catechism answer any of us might give, if we reflect honestly on our expectations, we shall probably have to admit to a dogged persistent expectation that no sort of argument will remove: the expectation that things should make sense in this world of our everyday experience. We know it does not always happen that way. We watch honest businessmen fail and dishonest ones prosper; good landlords grow poor and mean ones become millionaires; charitable people die of cancer while yet young; careful, considerate people killed by drunken drivers; and similar tragedies. Yet every time something like this happens we feel outraged, stunned, bewildered. It ought not to be. It offends our sense of a good and all-powerful God.

This spontaneous reaction is not at all unchristian. Rather, it lies very close to the heart of the Christian message of hope. That message is of Jesus Christ, the Messiah, the promised one who brings the time of salvation, the Reign of God. The preaching of the Apostles refers back to the preaching of Jesus himself.

Jesus had said that the Kingdom of Heaven was at hand, that the promised Reign of God could be now, right away, if men would simply open their hearts to the possibility of it. But in the Sermon on the Mount and elsewhere in the gospels we have a record of what he said were the conditions for the Reign of God Clearly, the challenge was too much for his listeners. They could not trust him that much. They would not risk that much. They could not bring themselves to be that generous. His presence and his message made them so uncomfortable that eventually enough people agreed he had to be "gotten rid of."

On the surface of it, that had to be the end. He had said, "The Reign of God can be now, if you trust me," but they did not trust him. He had said his own life was the pledge of it, but his life ended in disaster. It seemed as though no good news of hope could possibly be salvaged from that. That is exactly what the Apostles at first concluded, namely that it had all been a very beautiful dream, but utter illusion. Then an experience happened, the details of which we shall never quite know, because the Apostles themselves used such mysterious and poetic language to describe it. What we do know is that it happened to many of them. It changed their lives totally, and the impact of it has carried the followers of Jesus through twenty centuries and many culture changes and innumerable persecutions, none of which has been able to submerge their vision or their hope that the Reign of God is at hand.

To make any sense of Christianity at all, one must ask what is meant by the Reign of God, or the other term for it, the Kingdom of Heaven. Jesus seems not to have explained what he meant by it. His followers, at least, have not recorded any definition. What they have left us are many parables that give hints how the Reign of God comes about. What it is is taken for granted, just as what is meant by God is taken for granted because it was an important element in existing Jewish thought, writing, worship and life.

In the history of the Jews the early period of the monarchy came at a time when it was very difficult to hold the nation together, and the kings were the champions who did this. The people's experience of kings was that they were saviors of the nation. But that soon changed as the kings abused their power and prophets took up the cry that the kingship (or royal rule) of Israel really belonged to God and that the king rules only within the rule of God. A tension arose, which Jesus was later to recall and emphasize, between the true reign of God whose law is written in men's hearts, and the reign of the kings of the earth who lord it over their subjects, make them pay taxes, draft them into the army, and use power over their subjects to enrich themselves.

Because of the legends and loyalties that were entwined around the dynasty of David, it was not surprising that, as the kingdom disintegrated, David was the symbol used to project the hope of Israel forward. The prophets looked at the sin and suffering and confusion in Israel with unabashed conviction that God, who delivered Israel out of Egypt, and who was the true sovereign of all the world, the maker of all with power over all, would be sure to fulfill his promise of ruling over Israel himself with justice and peace. They expressed this by saying that a descendant of the house of David would mount the throne and really reign one day as God's deputy.

In the course of time, Israel fell into so many misfortunes that it took great and deep faith to look into the future with hope that God would still fulfill his promise. Projections of this promise became more mysterious and more poetic in tone. A pattern emerged of expecting a savior king, a champion, an anointed one who would come at the end of history and before the Reign of God, which he would somehow prepare and usher in. This was Messiah or "the Christ." The figure of Messiah in prophecy and popular expectation was always rather ambiguous. It was not, for instance, clear that only one such person was expected. Neither was it clear whether he was expected to be a military and political or merely spiritual leader. As we know, at the time of Jesus the popular expectation leaned heavily towards a spectacular military leader. In any case, the expectation was that the Messiah would establish a reign of justice and peace, that his rule would be genuinely a human rule within the rule of God, and that eventually he would turn over to God completely his kingship and his power so that God would reign directly, an idea that is echoed in the first chapter of the letter to the Ephesians and the first chapter of the letter to the Colossians.

If the figure of Messiah was mysterious, much more so was the Reign of God he was to usher in. The Jewish people were as scandalized and outraged as any of us today when they noticed that the wicked often prospered and that powerful people used their power not for the common good but to oppress the weak. If the God who brought them out of Egypt was the Lord of all and faithful to his promises, it was a contradiction that those who kept his law should suffer for it. Keeping his law ought to ensure that things went right.

It led them to the conviction that the Exodus from Egypt in the past was the hint and promise of what was yet to come, when God would vindicate his faithful. They took the analogy of the savior kings and asserted that God himself would be the savior king of Israel in the future. But they also set up a contrast between the inadequacy of all earthly reigns and the perfect Reign of God. When God reigns it is not like the rulers of the earth who lord it over their subjects to take advantage of them and enrich themselves, for the Reign of God is entirely for the welfare of those over whom he reigns. God's law is not like the laws of the kings of the earth, because kings guarantee their laws by sanctions that are external to the purpose of the laws, fear of punishment, while the sanction of God's law is its inner wisdom and truth.

The prophets spoke of the Reign of God in highly poetic terms. In that day, when all the nations will gather around Jerusalem worshipping the one God, who will reign from his holy mountain, lions will lie down with lambs, the land will yield abundance of harvests, men will be busy converting their weapons of war into constructive tools. Any further discussion never translates this poetic language into a literal description. It suggests only that the point of the poetic language is to hint at the fulfillment of men's deepest desires or longings. What is much clearer is what the Reign of God is not. There will be no more war, poverty, oppression of the weak, sickness, fear or suffering.

The reason for the vagueness of the accounts of the Reign of God is quite obviously that it is impossible to know much about it, because all admit that what they are talking about is beyond anything we have seen or heard or even dreamed of. The understanding of it must grow with the experience of moving closer to it. That is probably why, in the period between the last of the Hebrew Scriptures and the life of Jesus, it was the practice of the rabbis to teach about the Reign of God in two different ways. They would exhort the individual to accept the Reign of God in his own life, to live by the law of God, to judge all other laws and all other authorities by that of God. Of course, if everyone did this, the Reign of God would come simply because all the affairs of men would be directed to God in justice and peace and compassion.

But the great scandal is that, if most people do not do it, the man who does suffers. People may simply take advantage of his honesty, courtesy, generosity. Or they may find him a threat because his life is a constant challenge to injustice and deceit and greed and because he may find that in the name of the kingship of God he must speak up against the misuse of power by earthly rulers. In this case he may be actively persecuted even to death. And the Jewish people had plenty of experience of that.

In response to this scandal, the rabbis taught that the Reign of God would one day be manifest with great power. God himself would vindicate his people and the just man would triumph because the wisdom and the plan of God would be fully revealed. God would come swiftly; he would come when he was ready. There was more than a hint in this way of preaching that the promise of the coming Reign of God would make sense only to those who now took upon themselves the yoke of the kingdom of God. If you look at what is going on in the world, you might be so discouraged that you would assume that God either does not care or else is not all-powerful. Otherwise he would come crashing in and demolish the evildoers and set the scene right. If, however, you reflect on your own life and your life is one of trying to bring about justice, making peace and acting from compassion, you realize that God is much more like this and works from within men's consciences and from within their freedom.

Of course, that left another question, about the fate of those who lived and worked and suffered to bring about the Reign of God and then died before it happened. Long before the time of Jesus it was already customary to speak poetically about God awakening the departed just from their sleep of death to participate in the fulfillment of God's promises. It was a popular expectation that when the Messiah arrived to usher in the Reign of God, the bodies of the just would rise from their graves and share in the rejoicing.

Before, during, and after the life of Jesus, there was controversy whether the Messiah would be a spiritual or a politico-military leader, and whether the Reign of God would be a political theocracy or some sort of spiritual realm. When Jesus said the Kingdom of Heaven was at hand, some people may really have thought that he meant he would lead a military uprising against the Roman colonial occupation and was calling people to follow him and take up arms.

Jesus went to great pains to distinguish himself from that school of thought, but there is no testimony that he said the Kingdom of Heaven meant only another "place" after death, or that the Kingdom of Heaven was simply a matter of private attitudes of individual people, not related to transforming the real world around us with its sin and suffering and oppressive use of power. If he had wanted to explain that the Kingdom of Heaven, or Reign of God, would not solve the scandal of the injustice of this world but only draw people's minds away from being preoccupied with it, he would have had to say this quite explicitly and the Apostles would have had to record it quite explicitly in order to show how the hope that Jesus held out differed from the expectation of Israel. He could not have used the same words and expected the people to know he meant something quite different without ever explaining as much.

Then as now, people were quite shocked by the radical nature of the message of Jesus. Perhaps they could envisage changes in the power structures of the world coming about only through more bloodshed and more oppression and violence and fear of punishment. Then rightly they might conclude that that would bring the promise of the Reign of God, which is without force and fear, no nearer. But Jesus speaks as one who follows the rabbinic teaching to take upon oneself the yoke of the Reign of God, and he invites his followers to do the same. At the same time he expresses radical demands for the bringing about of the Kingdom, for instance those in the Sermon on the Mount, and only hints how God will in fact establish that Kingdom, for instance in the many parables of the Kingdom of Heaven, which he does not want to explain further. This is in the same rabbinic tradition. There is no point in giving any kind of logically persuasive explanation how the Kingdom will really happen in order to persuade people to commit themselves to it. He can only hope to coax them into some kind of genuine commitment because the understanding of what it is all about, and how the world can be redeemed and transformed into the Reign of God, has to grow out of the experience within that commitment. This may be why, instead of beginning with a clear statement of his platform and then asking people to join him, Jesus, as we meet him in the gospels, seems to make his one basic demand that of discipleship, of learning from him by following him, which many people find distressingly imprecise.

Even today, people object to mixing religion and politics, or religion and economics. They would like the sphere of religion carefully defined and kept separate, with the demands and conditions clearly and explicitly set out. But those who ask this may still admit that under it all they are outraged by the injustices of the world as it is, because a good and all-powerful God should not allow it. They may hope that if individual believers observe their religious duties, God will intervene and put things right in His own good time. But this was not the understanding of the Reign of God which Jesus took over from his tradition and did not contradict. In that understanding God reigns from within men's conscience and from within their freedom and not by overwhelming them from without. Therefore, He is constantly inviting us to set right our unjust world in whatever way we can as our experience and our understanding grows. Discipleship, the learning from Jesus and following him, cannot be spelt out in an explicit set of commandments or instructions, because our understanding how to set the world right and bring about the Reign of God must grow out of the practice of discipleship in our twentieth century world.

The Church's teaching has incorporated in the creeds the same paradox, the same invitation and the same hinting quality that characterized the description of our hope which Jesus took over from the rabbinic tradition. We express our belief in the rising again of the dead and the life of a world yet to come. And we know that there is no point in explaining what we mean by that because one can only get nearer to understanding it by taking on oneself the yoke of the Reign of God, by following Jesus in discipleship.

NOTES

The idea of the Reign of God in the New Testament writings has been set out in great detail in *God's Rule and Kingdom* by Rudolf Schnackenburg (Herder and Herder, 1966). The biblical phrases and their meaning at different times are traced very carefully in *Bible Key Words*, Vol. II, ed. Gerhard Kittel (Harper & Row, 1958), but this work is quite technical.

The problems of hope connected with our individual future and destiny are discussed further in Chapters 3, 5 and 6. The problems connected with social action and hope for the future and destiny of the world are discussed further in the last two chapters of this book.

CHAPTER III—THE GOD OF OUR FAITH

As has already been mentioned, Christian faith starts out by taking God for granted and claiming that he is revealed to us as merciful, reconciling all things to himself in Jesus Christ, his Son. At the core of the Christian faith there is no speculation about God; there is an experience of having met God and having been overwhelmed and overjoyed by it.

The Christian understanding of God does not begin from a philosophical definition of God and then proceed to decide how he should be worshipped and whether he may have revealed himself. It begins from the worship of the God who has revealed himself to the community and from there, every now and then, answers the philosophical questions that are put to it. Christian tradition is not a philosophy but a life. What we hand on from generation to generation is an experience of God's grace in our lives and a way of life that is a response to that grace. Only when it helps this process, does the Church engage in discussions and formulations of what exactly we mean by God. More often that not, what emerges is an identification of those things that are not God but idols, or a careful statement of what God is not like, or a recalling of the biblical stories and images.

The picture that an outsider puts together is that this is a hidden God, an elusive God. This is not an incorrect picture, because Christians do not claim to know God directly but to see a sort of faint mirror image. We claim to see God reflected in his wonderful works in the world of nature and in history, and most of all we claim to see him reflected in the man Jesus— in what he was, in what he did, and in what he suffered.

Before the creeds were formulated, the early Christians had already had to explain twice what God was not. They were at pains to make it clear in their preaching and in the gospels that God as reflected in Jesus was not much interested in ritual and elaborate prayers, but was concerned with the values by which people lived their everyday lives and in particular with unselfishness, compassion for the needy and oppressed, and care for the common welfare. He was not a God of ceremonies, and observances, and consecrated holy places, but a God to be worshipped in spirit and in truth. One might say, in this sense, that God as presented by Jesus is a radically secular God, interested in all the practical affairs of the world and not content to be relegated to Sabbath, temple, and synagogue, or to Sunday and church and ecclesiastical affairs.

A second issue the early Christians had to clarify was that God as revealed in Jesus is not a partisan God. He was not a God of Jews more than gentiles, of the civilized or cultured peoples rather than the barbarians, of the free rather than of slaves, or of men, as though women were only subsidiary human beings. Quite to the contrary, in the cross of Jesus all these opposites are reconciled, and believers learn that the God they seek and serve is equally concerned with the destiny of all men—with Communists individually and collectively as much with the industrial capitalist societies, with persons of all races, all ages, both sexes, all creeds, all political persuasions. The God we worship will not take our side against other human persons because he cares about them too much. He will not take our side when we try to kill, injure, or impoverish other peoples. What we learn from Jesus is rather that in such cases God is the champion of the poor, the suffering, the oppressed.

God takes our side only when we realize that the struggle is not against other people but against the superhuman grip of evil, against crushing systems where everyone seems to have lost control and injustice perpetuates itself, against an atmosphere of fear and distrust in which everyone sees the other as a threat and an imminent aggressor, against a general sense of helplessness in the face of evil, against a silent assumption that religious and moral questions must be kept out of public decision-making.

Israel had struggled with these questions long before the time of Jesus. When the time came for Christians to explain their understanding of God in their creeds, the best way was still to appeal to the Hebrew Scriptures and Jewish tradition. They described God as "the almighty Father, maker of heaven and earth" in the Apostles' Creed. In the Nicene Creed this is further elaborated in this fashion: "the one God, almighty Father, the maker of heaven and earth and of all things both visible and invisible."

That the description as Father should come first is natural to the whole tradition because it was the favorite term used by Jesus for the transcendent God. To call God Father implies intimacy, the possibility of a personal relationship, the proper possibility of praying. It implies providence. God cares for each human person and for mankind. Christians do not see themselves surrounded by blind fate, or caught up in great impersonal forces, or helpless in the face of history. They see themselves being invited to share in shaping their own future in response to God who cares for each of them personally.

To call God Father implies that we human beings are like God and are meant to grow more like him—like him who is concerned for all men in a personal way and does not play favorites, like him who creates and blesses and gives life, like him who is the Master of the universe, the Lord of history, the power and promise of the future. To call God Father also implies that he is the hidden source of our life. If one takes the biological analogy of fatherhood seriously, fatherhood is not directly experienced by the child but inferred from the way his father deals with him. Biologically, fatherhood is hidden from experience while motherhood is experienced concretely.

This image of the warm, personal, concerned but still-hidden God is matched with the description "all-powerful." We know from what can be traced of the history of the creeds that the original understanding was probably not so much that of an almighty Father, but of God, the Father, the Almighty, putting together two different titles for God taken from Jewish practice. In the course of time, Christians put the titles together to speak of the Almighty Father. This is not strange, for Christians see God's power as manifested chiefly in his fatherhood of all men in creation, and of Jesus Christ as savior of the world, of those who call him father in the name of Jesus, sharing thereby in a special way the special sonship of Jesus.

The Father of Our Lord, Jesus Christ, is revealed as powerful, not by throwing thunderbolts, crashing down in judgment upon the evildoer. He does not even work a mighty miracle to prevent the criminal execution of Jesus. He does not overwhelm men's freedom. His power works within men's freedom, not against it to curtail or crush it. It is the power of a limitless self-gift of life and truth and grace which is powerful because of its intrinsic desirability, powerful because it makes sense and gives happiness.

The notion that God is almighty is closely related to the experience that God is faithful. This was perhaps the most basic description of God in Jewish teaching and the Hebrew Scriptures. The Bible often describes God as being in a covenant relationship with all men and with Israel in particular. By this it means that God has given a promise on which He will never turn His back, even if men do not observe their side of the agreement. It was and is the custom of the Jewish people to reflect on the great experiences of liberation and hope of the past, and to try to understand what God was saying to them in those events.

The most important of these was the Exodus from Egypt. Israel reflected on that year by year through the centuries, at the Passover seder and also at other times. The people realized that in the Exodus they had been called and inspired and helped to break through immovable barriers to human dignity and freedom and peoplehood and justice. When their sufferings had become so bad that they were up against sheer despair, the call of God broke in on them through their representative, Moses. They did not know who God was, what God was like, what his name was. All they knew was his powerful command to them to break through and come out of slavery. But that was all that it concerned them to know.

Moses knew that he was "called by name" by this hidden and mysterious God and that he had to answer. So Moses answered and obeyed, and the people eventually answered and obeyed, and their hope and faith were not betrayed. They emerged into freedom. When they reflected on it later, they realized that coming out of Egypt was not yet the definitive step to freedom. Yet along the way, when it appeared that they would die of famine or thirst, they found themselves providentially sustained. When it seemed that everything would break up from internal rivalries and strife, they were summoned again by the powerful call of God to accept his law so that they might live and really become one people, at Sinai. In spite of fearful odds, their faith and hope and courage and sheer dogged perseverance brought them finally into possession of the land they were convinced God had promised them.

In all of this they were looking at the events of their history and saw in them the providence and faithfulness of God, who had not challenged them to come out of Egypt in vain. The more they had responded to the call of God, the more sense it all made. They began to see the possibility of a final liberation from the consequences of evil deeds, from suffering and oppression. They saw this possibility in their own fidelity to the Law that God had revealed to them as his way and his wisdom.

As the Bible records for us, Israel, in fact, was by no means always faithful. Yet it was the experience of the Jewish people that through events, through their prophets, even through great catastrophes, they were always being confronted again with the call of God and his own wisdom held out to them in the Law by which they could survive and reach happiness. It seemed that the light and inspiration and gift of God were always there, no matter how long or how often the people turned away from it. They recognized God as eternally faithful, always waiting for them to begin again or to resume the work of redemption from suffering and from sin.

Israel expressed its experience of this fidelity in the idea of covenants—the covenant of creation, the covenant of Noah and the covenant of Abraham renewed with Moses and formally offered to and accepted by the whole people of Israel at Sinai. Israel recognized that the fidelity of God has roots in the physical universe. The sun rises and sets in predictable pattern;

the stars keep their course so that one can find one's way through the desert by their guidance at night; the moon waxes and wanes, measuring off the months; crops grow and ripen and wither and reseed themselves and grow again. If you plant, you can expect to harvest. If men study nature around them, it is not in vain. They are not betrayed. They find that there are laws of nature and that men can take possession of nature, of the earth, by learning those laws and observing them. Life and existence are not wholly irrational or chaotic or absurd. Life makes sense, and man is invited to keep on taking possession of it and make more sense out of it. The covenant of creation does not guarantee that life will be easy or without struggle, but it does guarantee that the world and life are not absurd.

The covenant of Noah refers to the story of the flood and the renewal of human life in the family of Noah, the just man, under the sign of the rainbow. It is concerned with the question whether it is worthwhile to be morally upright. It asserts that God takes care of those who live honestly, justly, compassionately, seeking to fulfill his law as they can discover it written in nature, though they may not have shared his revelation to Israel. The covenant of Noah is a colorful way of saying that there is a God and that he rewards the good and punishes the evil. In other words, God is faithful not only in nature, which works by observable laws, but also in history, in the affairs and conscience of men. He does not demand of men's consciences behavior which is nonsensical or which destroys life and hope. What he has written into consciences is the law of life, the law by which men may survive and prosper.

The covenant of Abraham and Moses and Sinai is

the special covenant of Israel to whom God has revealed himself. It is the covenant that God will be most intimately their God, revealing the inner wisdom of his laws to them so that they might be a witness to all mankind. At first, in the history of Israel, there was little reflection on the universal dimension of the choosing or election of the Jewish people. There was simply the overwhelming realization of the great and continuing liberation they had experienced and were experiencing, as the gift of a God who was always there to sustain them even when they forgot about him. That they should have been sought out or chosen this way was cause for great wonder, gratitude and hymns of praise. Only gradually, and mainly through the voices of the prophets, was it realized that such a special calling and election could never be at the expense of the rest of mankind but only for their service, because the God of the covenant of Abraham was the great universal God of the covenant of creation who renewed that covenant in a special way with Noah on behalf of all men of good will.

The Christian community saw the fidelity of God in a new covenant event—the rising of Jesus from the dead. For them that became the new and everlasting covenant, the definitive breakthrough of the overwhelming and compassionate faithfulness of God against all the sin and rejection of men. In the teaching and person of Jesus the faithfulness of God had taken on a very concrete and intimate presence. The Apostles had recognized it as the time of the fulfillment to which all the promises and all the covenants led. When the forces of the world aligned themselves against Jesus and decided he threatened too many established interests and was to be considered the enemy of society and executed, it seemed to the Apostles that the whole understanding of the faithfulness of the God of the covenants had been nothing more than wishful thinking. Hope had really been finally and forever swallowed by despair, and all meaning in life had simply disappeared into absurdity and chaos.

It is in this life that we have to try to understand the Resurrection as the seal of the faithfulness of God, as the final great sign or token of God's covenant with men, as the new and everlasting covenant. In the Apostles' experience, that faithfulness of God was revealed in a new and extraordinary way, because he did not intervene to overwhelm men by external force even when they executed Jesus. The self-gift of God continues triumphant even over death, yet still as a gift freely offered to be freely accepted. They record for us that Jesus was seen again in great clarity, glorified, having passed through death to the life of the world to come. But he was seen only by those who believed in him, only by those who sought him. There was no miracle, no spectacular scene to compel acknowledgment from those who did not believe in him. That was not the way of the Father with men and it was not the way of Jesus.

This definitive self-revelation of God in Jesus leaves God as hidden as before, still recognized not by seeing him face to face but by reflecting on his works in nature and history, still to be sought only by faith, still characterized mainly by his faithfulness. This faithfulness is constantly attested by individual believers. Yet it remains as mysterious with them as it does with the tradition as a whole. A man or woman who has suffered a great deal in life, has been treated unjustly, been a victim of disease or natural disaster or great social calamities, will often assert with great assurance that God is faithful to those who seek him.

This obviously does not refer to ordinary prosperity, to being kept from suffering or harm or loss, or being rewarded with success in business or a profession. It refers to a much expanded consciousness of what human life is about, what makes people happy. It refers to the reflection of the faithfulness of God within the faithfulness of the believer himself, whose awareness of reality begins to grasp in some depth and breadth the covenant relationship of man to God. Because it is rooted in his own most intimate experience, that conviction is not easily shaken by experiences of adversity. And because it is drawn from the practice of a life of faith, it is not comprehensible to the unbeliever, that is, to the person who does not live by faith. That is why the Bible warns us that the witnesses to the covenant fidelity of God have been ridiculed ever since Noah and Abraham. That is why the Bible presents us with the riddle of Job.

NOTES

Most of the descriptive account of the Christian understanding of God in this chapter is drawn directly from the Epistles of Paul in the New Testament and from Genesis and Exodus in the Hebrew Scriptures.

The question of the relation between philosophy's understanding of God and the religious understanding is discussed at length and most helpfully in *The Other Dimension* by Louis Dupre (Macmillan, 1972), a difficult but very rewarding book.

The Jewish understanding of God, which Christians have accepted and taken for granted from the beginning, is beautifully presented in *God in Search of Man* by Abraham Joshua Heschel (Harper Torchbook, 1967).

There is relatively little written on the Christian doctrine of God, because it is usually taken for granted, while the focus is on Jesus as the revelation of God.

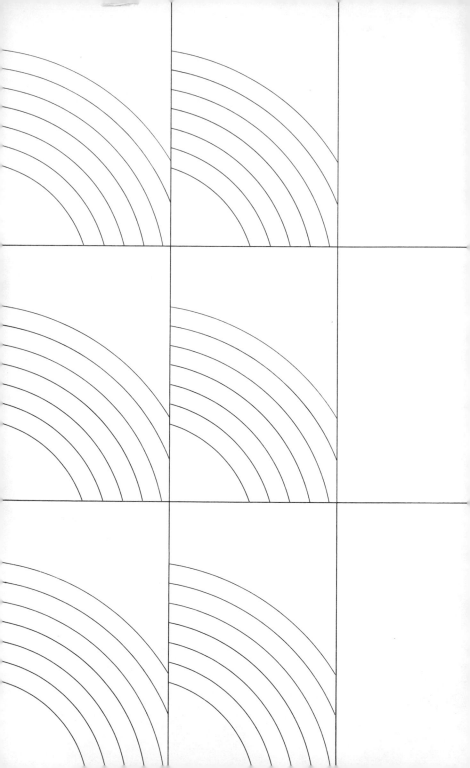

CHAPTER IV—CREATION AND SIN

The creeds identify God as creator or maker of heaven and earth and of all things visible or invisible. As in the Jewish tradition long before, Christians found it necessary to make a special point about the relation of man and the world and all things that exist to the God Christians worship. There are probably several reasons for this, but the principal one seems to be the problem of evil.

It is not immediately evident to any casual observer that there is one God who is master of the universe and all its powers and forces, and who also cares very much about the happiness of men. It is not evident because of the many hazards and dangers of life in the world, because of disease and natural disasters and death. It is not evident because of the natural enmity even among the animals, many of whom live by killing one another, and because of the apparently inevitable competition among men for the means of livelihood.

The more likely perception of the casual observer is that at the beginning there is chaos, that most of the forces of nature are quite out of everybody's control, that survival is a savage struggle for man and beast in which the strongest and the most relentlessly cruel win. It seems that the only thing that ever reduces the hazards and sets any boundaries to the chaos is the ruthless elimination of weaker species and the banding together of common interest groups. But even then, as great writers have been pointing out from the classical Greek tragedies down to such authors as Camus in our own day, in the end chaos wins because even the victor dies and never really has power to harmonize all the warring forces in nature and among men. Even wise and privileged people, living in times of relative peace and order and civilization, have looked around them and concluded that life is absurd—that there is no meaning given and that man's effort to make meaning is, in the end, always doomed to failure.

If some of us are not immediately struck with the apparent truth of these observations, it is probably because we are among the rare persons in the history of the world who have been sheltered from looking at raw chaos. This is only possible in certain highly developed industrial societies, in brief periods free of depressions and disasters, when there is no direct exposure to war and death-dealing epidemics. Even then, it is only possible for those in the society who are relatively wealthy, middle or upper class, not unemployed, not suffering from incurable disease, not struggling through a marriage that is falling apart, not despised for their race or other personal qualities, not suffering from drug addiction or alcoholism in the family, not having lost any close relative by war or crime or accident, not yet face to face with death. But most people have to ask, "Why? why? How can such a thing happen? What is the meaning of it?" and receive absolutely no answer. The advice of unbelieving friends is to take a cruise, get drunk, have the doctor prescribe a sedative, forget the past and concentrate on the future, make up your mind that this is the way it is and there are no answers, no reasonable hopes for justice, peace, fulfillment of man's yearnings. Frequently it is treated as a problem of adjustment, but adjustment to what? To chaos? To meaninglessness, hopelessness?

This is where the believer really has another answer. In the face of all the apparently contradictory evidence, he confesses that there is one God, the creator of men and of the universe, who indeed knows what he is doing and brings all things to a meaningful consummation. The story of creation in Genesis and the doctrine that developed from it were not really concerned with when or how things began, or whether there was a beginning of time before which there was no time and there were no things. It was not a theory of the universe, a philosophical cosmology. It was a very practical response to the difficulties sketched above.

Today when we think of the creation, our minds tend to jump at once to the idea of making something come into existence out of nothing. The biblical word used was a special, sacred word that did not really have any secular equivalents, but it was used eventually not only for the Genesis story but for God's action in bringing Israel into existence as a people and in bringing about his reign on earth. When it was translated into Greek a word was used that pertains to the founding of a city. When Christians translated it into Latin they also used a word that really had to do with begetting or fathering. This word became the more common, and "create" is the English form for it. It is not accidental that we speak of creativity in relation to art and sometimes in relation to human relationships and social structure. When we describe a person as creative we mean that that person seems to generate out of inner resources new possibilities, new realities, a new beginning, a new world. Great scientists are creative because they see relationships and connections that were not seen before and out of that vision a new thing, perhaps a whole new civilization arises, as with the wheel and with steam power.

This is closely related to the idea of creation in Genesis. The story does not tell of making out of nothing but of making out of chaos, confusion, darkness, wild and destructive flood waters. God separates the unruly waters, assigns them boundaries so that there is a space in between where things can begin to grow and live and flourish. He shines light into the darkness so that it is possible to see what is going on there. He gives the sea to the fishes, the air to the birds, the earth to the four-footed creatures. He makes man a creator like himself, breathes his own breath of life into him, and turns him around toward the earth out of which he came, to see, and understand and take possession and continue the work of creation.

It is because of this conception of the making of order out of chaos that the word for creation carries over so easily into the founding of Israel as a people. Here again man is the co-creator of the society that reflects God. It now became possible for men to seek God as their true end. Here again the creation is described as a making out of chaos, out of rivalries, enmities, distrust and selfishness, in which no one can survive.

It is because of this conception of creation, furthermore, as being the making of sense and peace and harmony out of chaos, that creation appears as unfinished, as always still taking place in the present and suggesting long perspectives into the future. The completion of creation will be the building of the Reign of God among men. And this is not a purely spiritual matter—that is, a non-material, non-secular task. It is indeed the completion of creation with the concern to find food and decent housing and peace and cures for disease for all.

The Christian doctrine of creation asserts that in the beginning and in the end it is God who creates and that his design transcends all men's plans and vision and history itself in a consummation so far beyond what we have seen or heard that we cannot imagine it.

At the same time we assert that God makes man in his own image and likeness, that, in a special way, God fathers mankind, to co-create with him. And we assert that God is the creator both of heaven and of earth, of all things seen and unseen. We do not, and cannot, as Christians, assume that there are forces or elements of reality and of the world in which we live which escape the power of God and cannot be brought to the consummation of creation—whether they be political, economic, social or natural forces. The savior God is the founder of the whole, the master of the universe, the Lord of history. But his Lordship is exercised within the freedom of men who are in his image.

In this context it becomes quite clear why the early Christians began to speak of Jesus Christ as the key to creation. It is in him that we can discern the design of creation. He is seen as the original "pattern" in which creation takes shape, because he can be the cornerstone making all things one in harmony so that he will indeed be able to turn over his reign or leadership to the Reign of God, and all things will be reconciled to their true end. Jesus offers us a vision of the goal and a perspective for striving towards that goal, because in the name of Jesus the powers of heaven and earth, the things seen and unseen, bow and recognize the Lordship of God and the ultimate meaning emerging out of the chaos.

This, of course, is not a descriptive statement of what has already happened, but a prophetic assertion of what Christians can see shaping up within the present chaos in the world. It is a faith statement, not based upon simple observation looking out into a world seen as object, but based rather on reflection upon the conversion that the believer has experienced within himself and within the community of believers, which gives him a new and creative vision of the possibilities for the world at large. The Christian confession of faith in God as creator and in Jesus as the cornerstone of creation, the new Adam, is also a commitment to participate in that creative process.

The creeds do not explicitly relate creation and sin, possibly because to earlier generations of Christians the connection was obvious and they could simply proceed to explain their belief in Jesus as the Christ saving men from sin. Or it may simply have been that every article of our creed is so closely linked to every other that not all the connections can be made clear. Whichever it may be, the fact remains that creation is also partly a confession of faith when confronted with the consequences of evil deeds. It is not only a creation out of chaos, moving through history with a struggle, and ending gloriously after a steady climb through an evolutionary process. The creation that our Christian doctrine describes is one disrupted and broken myriad times by sin, so that the progress to the end is not only a task of creation. It is also a task of redemption or liberation, to set mankind and the world free from the consequences of evil deeds, so that the ascent to the Reign of God is possible.

The Bible does not give us definitions of sin, much less an explanation of how sin is possible. It simply tells stories of sin and the consequences of sin, and these stories are full of explosive symbolism that suggests so much more than they actually spell out. There are stories of killing, deception, lust, greed. They are all related to the first quite mysterious story of sin, in which the man and the woman attempt to take that which belongs only to God and thereby destroy their own integrity and harmony, so that they no longer really have a home on the earth. The garden of paradise, a kind of original harmony and simplicity, is destroyed, and there is no return to it. The re-entry is barred by an angel with a flaming sword. There can be salvation only by moving on, out into the world, into history, into the task of dealing with the consequences of evil deeds.

For both Jewish tradition and Christian tradition, sin is a mystery. It is a mystery how sin is possible if there is an all-powerful creator God. It would not be possible at all, because the idea would simply not make sense, if there were no God. If existence has a purpose, if men have a true end, if there is a design for the harmony of all things, then to reject this purpose, this design is evil, is sin. If life is absurd and there is no one ultimate goal or purpose, no possibility of fulfillment for the world as a whole and for all mankind, then any goal that an individual chooses to pursue is only relatively good or bad, depending on the point of view from which you look at it. Killing people becomes a good idea if you win a trading advantage by it. It is not, of course, a good idea from the point of view of the people being killed, but you may not have any particular reason to be looking at the question from their point of view. In self defense, people may eventually get around to an agreement or law that all killing is forbidden, but in that case killing becomes only illegal, not sinful.

To understand what it meant by sin, one must have faith in one God, in whom it all makes sense, and one must have some experience of what the fullness of life directed towards that one God can be. Israel claimed this out of the Sinai covenant, the experience of being one people called by God and oriented to God. Out of the revelation of the Law, God's wisdom and purpose shared with them, they recognized sin for what it was.

Christians claim that out of the new covenant in the blood of Jesus, out of the revelation in the person of Jesus, God's love and purpose shared with us, we recognize sin for what it is. We look into the world where the unbeliever sees chaos and absurdity, and we see sin—for instance, in poverty where it need not be, in discrimination among races and peoples who are all children of one God, in war as a means used by power groups to settle disputes that are not even of interest to ordinary people who are killed and wounded and deprived of their homes.

Where the unbeliever looks and concludes that the world has always been like this because men's interests are necessarily in conflict and they will resolve the conflicts by force, the Christian looks and remembers the vision he has seen in Jesus Christ how the world is supposed to be. He concludes that in the beginning it was not so, that God made a world and it was good, fashioned people and they were good, but sin intervened. He knows that sin intervened because in the light of Christ he knows himself as a sinner, as one who does not live fully oriented to God, and therefore out of his experience he recognizes the consequences of sin for what they are.

Of course, this "in the beginning," as in Genesis, does not really refer to a starting point in time. It refers rather to the principle of creation, the foundation of existence in the world which is not absurd, or rotten or bad, but good. For a Christian this also refers to Jesus Christ who is the principle, or pattern, or beginning of creation. When we see him as the principle or design of creation, we know him as the great peacemaker who is Son of God, the prince of peace, and we know that war and oppression and impoverishment of the weak are not inevitable, not written into the pattern of creation but are the consequences of sin, many times compounded. We also know that in Jesus Christ we can be set free from the consequences of sin no matter how many times compounded, that the world has not somehow rolled away out of God's control.

The freedom from sin, the redemption, however, is a gift that must be freely accepted. This is the other aspect of the mystery of sin—that man can oppose God, that the power of the all-powerful God works in men's freedom and not against it. This is difficult enough to understand even in relation to the person who sins, but it raises a further question about the providence of God when related to the victims of the sin. It would sometimes seem that men can curtail the power of God in relation to other men whom they oppress not only in body but in mind, in their very concept of themselves and in their very freedom. It is only a personal commitment to and participation in the work of the redemption that can come to grips with this particular paradox. It cannot be done by thinking alone.

In the Christian interpretation of the biblical stories of sin, there developed the idea of original sin as a state of existence into which we are born, bearing the consequences of evil deeds to which we were not party. The purpose of this doctrine is not to make people feel guilty for the sins that were committed before their time, but rather to persuade them to accept the common responsibility for putting right a state of affairs that ought not to be. As a Christian, I cannot absolve myself of responsibility for racial discrimination in housing or schooling, simply because I am not the one who brought it about. I am not to blame, but I am responsible for finding remedies. Neither can I absolve myself of responsibility for my country's wars just because I did not declare them. I am not to blame but I must find ways to make peace. I am probably not to blame for the poverty around me, but I am responsible for finding ways of building a more just society.

Sin in the Christian understanding is a very broad concept, because it includes all that is discerned as evil in the light of Christ and the promise of the Reign of God.

NOTES

As in the last chapter, most of the material here is based on the scriptures, particularly Genesis and the letters of St. Paul.

A very careful historical study of the Christian doctrine of creation and providence is available in *Creation and Providence,* by Leo Scheffczyk (Herder and Herder, 1970), but it is detailed and not easy reading.

A good discussion of the Christian understanding of sin is available in *Man and Sin* by Piet Schoonenberg (University of Notre Dame Press, 1968).

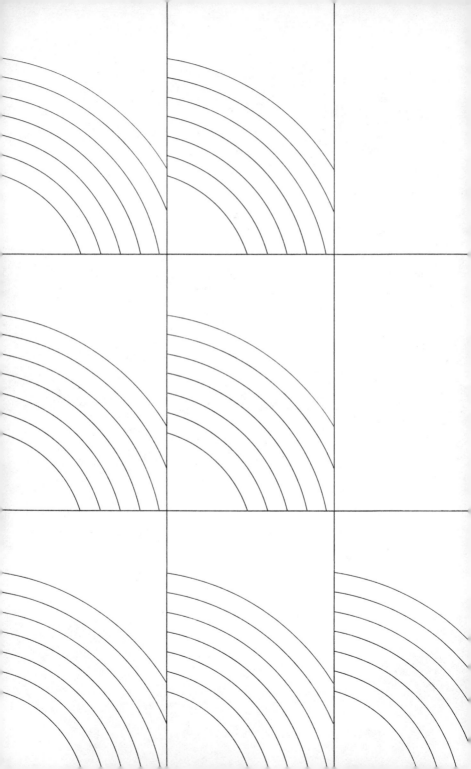

CHAPTER V—JESUS AS LIBERATOR OF MANKIND

As was mentioned in the first chapter, the second section of the creed, concerning Jesus, is the core of the Christian confession of faith. In the Apostles' Creed we affirm our faith in Jesus Christ, God's only Son, our Lord, who was conceived by the Holy Spirit, born of the Virgin Mary, suffered under Pontius Pilate, was crucified, died and was buried. We further affirm that he descended into hell, that on the third day he rose again, that he ascended into heaven and sits at the right hand of the Father, whence he shall come to judge the living and the dead.

For most Christians today, this language is so strange and the message seems so unrelated to any social situation with which we are familiar, that a common response is not so much the Amen of "count me in on it," but rather a puzzled declaration that, because the Church teaches it, it must be true, though it is difficult to understand what it all means.

The account in the Nicene Creed does not help because it is even stranger to our ears. At the Sunday Eucharist we confess our faith in one Lord, Jesus Christ, the only-begotten Son of God, born of the Father, before all ages, God of God, Light of Light, true God of true God, begotten not made, of one substance with the Father, by whom all things were made. We then continue that for us men and for our salvation he came down from heaven and he became flesh by the Holy Spirit of the Virgin Mary and was made man, that he was also crucified for us, suffered under Pontius Pilate and was buried, that on the third day he rose again according to the scriptures, ascended into heaven and sits at the right hand of the Father, that he will come again in glory to judge the living and the dead, and of his kingdom there will be no end.

This is a very extraordinary recital, obviously compiled over a lengthy period of time in many layers, and in response to particular problems and arguments, some of which we have long forgotten. Yet this is the profession of faith we most commonly use in public worship, and most adult Catholics would like to know more about what it means.

Probably the first important obstacle to understanding it is the fact that in both accounts, but especially in the Nicene Creed, we are confronted with an eternal divine pre-existence of Jesus before we are given any indication of what he did that makes him savior of men and Messiah or Christ. Many people today have the impression that the message is supposed to tell us that because Jesus is divine he is the savior of men and that he was so serious about it that he stayed around long enough to be crucified. This was not really necessary because anything he did would have sufficed for the salvation of men, but there was some special advantage in it because it showed everyone how great the love of God was. Because of our too literal way of thinking, our loss of poetry and symbolism and our narrow concept of truth, we have really turned these assertions the wrong way around. If they are honest about it, those who have received the message in this way find they cannot really make sense of it, at least not the kind of sense that would totally change their lives.

As a matter of fact and history, the proclamation about Jesus was built up and fitted together in exactly the opposite direction from the order we have in the creeds. Once you follow this original order you can arrive at a far clearer understanding of what the confession of faith in Jesus meant and was intended to convey to newcomers. The apostolic message was first and foremost a message about the man Jesus whom the community had known and loved and lost out of their midst and who had been restored to them in such an extraordinary way that it transformed their understanding of who he was and what he was about.

The preaching seems to have begun with the startled cry that "he was alive." The first challenge to the preaching seems to have been to the effect, "How do you mean 'alive'? Did we not bury him?" The proclamation settled down into the form that Jesus rose and his followers had seen him alive and he had commissioned them to go out to preach the good news, or that God raised him from the dead on the third day as had been foretold. It appears that the Apostles did not need to explain to their fellow Jews what they were talking about when they said that Jesus rose or that God raised him from the dead on the third day. The resurrection of the dead was already part of the expectation of the messianic era. In other words, the Jews of that time were used to hearing the Pharisees preach that, when the Reign of God came, the good people who had died earlier would rise from their graves, would awaken from the sleep of death, to join in the rejoicing. It is true that the Sadducees objected to this teaching, but it was nevertheless a popular expectation.

When the Apostles preached to fellow Jews that Jesus had risen from the dead and that his followers had seen him and been commissioned to spread the news, the response was different from what it would be today. The immediate question that arose was not how it was possible that a person who was really dead could come back to life, or what that really meant. As a matter of fact, they were not as sure of themselves as we are, in relation to the biology of death and what are the irreversible symptoms. In any case, the

Apostles were clearly not saying he had revived to continue the same life, but that he had passed through death into the glorious life of the world to come. The real questions that fellow Jews would have were concerned with the arrival of the Reign of God. They questioned how the Reign of God could have come without any obvious public difference in life. The Roman occupation of the country had not been ended; there seemed to be no less injustice or suffering or confusion in the world. Because the expectation of the messianic time was that the Kingship of God over all the earth would be publicly manifest, most Jews were quite scandalized when the Apostles preached that the Reign of God had already begun in Jesus who had risen from the dead.

There was another reason it was shocking. Jesus had been rejected as a false pretender and a danger to the people by the official leadership. Now his followers were preaching his resurrection as the "first-born from the dead," claiming that he ushered in the Reign of God, and therefore that he was Messiah. It was a problem how anyone who had died by criminal execution could ever be Messiah, that is, Christ, the one anointed by God to take final possession of the throne of David. If he had died in a victorious battle to set Israel free from foreign oppression, it would have been easier to understand. But he had not apparently achieved anything. He had not been executed by the Romans over the protests of the Jews, but with the approval of the leaders. It would have been almost impossible for Jews who were not already followers of Jesus and had not been involved in the experience of the resurrection to accept the message that Jesus had risen and was Messiah. It was an essential part of the very definition of Messiah that he had to be acknowledged as such by Israel. Jesus had not only not been acknowledged but officially rejected. This situation would be like asking a Catholic today to believe that the Pope and all the Bishops in Council had made a mistake about the most central issue in Christian doctrine.

Under these circumstances, it is extraordinary that the Apostles gained thousands of Jewish converts within a very short space of time. It is not extraordinary that many of these were strangers to Jerusalem and even to Palestine as a whole, who had come there on pilgrimage or had met the Apostles elsewhere. For them the scandal might be a little less; they would expect explosive prophetic events in Jerusalem, and their longing for the Messiah was so great because they lived in exile and earnestly waited for the whole world to become the place of God.

As the preaching moved farther away in time and space from the events, it was not enough to announce that Jesus had risen from the dead and therefore was the Christ. The new question that arose was, simply, who was Jesus? It was a request for an ordinary human, historical identification. The answer was that he was a Jew, born of someone the community had known, Mary, and that he had been arrested, tortured and executed under Pontius Pilate. There was no doubt that he had died, because he had been buried for several days. Matthew's gospel added that the tomb was guarded.

Neither the creeds nor the apostolic preaching as it is reported for us in the Acts of the Apostles really tell us why the death and resurrection of Jesus make him the Christ, or savior of the world. Yet the catechumen is obviously asked to do more than give an intellectual assent to the truth of the proposition. In the catechesis of the early centuries, the catechumen is asked to repent and be baptized, to be reborn into a new life by receiving the gift of the Holy Spirit and living in discipleship, that is, as one who is constantly learning from Jesus Christ by the light and understanding that the Holy Spirit gives.

Although this is the most important part of the message, because it explains what the believer is supposed to do and how he is supposed to live as a believer, it is the least explicitly spelt out. We have to read it and reflect on it in the gospel chapters concerned with the teaching of Jesus, beginning with his radical platform in the Sermon on the Mount, observing how Jesus deals with individuals in the many gospel stories of particular encounters, trying to understand John's summary of it in the Last Supper discourse (beginning with Chapter 13 of John's gospel), observing how the communities of the followers of Jesus lived, as described in the accounts in the Acts of the Apostles and in the Letters of the New Testament.

What is very clear from the beginning is that there were different styles of discipleship but some issues which were so basic that they were argued out until there was unanimity. For instance, it appears that a type of commune-style living in which property was held in common was thought of as very desirable but not required of everyone, whereas any type of racial or class discrimination (such as that between Hebrew- and Greek-speaking people, or between rich and poor at the Eucharistic gathering) was absolutely intolerable among Christians because it contradicted the very core of the Christian faith and commitment. It has been the Catholic claim through the centuries that the Spirit is with the Church, leading us to understand in changing circumstances what the teaching of Jesus means in practice, so as to continue the task of redemption "until he comes again," that is, until it is fulfilled and the Reign of God is publicly manifest to all.

Church teaching has always given us some guidance on this, because simply by reading the gospel one might be quite confused as to what discipleship of Jesus entails. The earliest generations did not learn it first or mainly from the gospels, but from participation in the living community, some members of which had known Jesus or known those who were friends of Jesus. They shared in the way of life that was handed on and which could never be adequately formulated in words.

Even with the help of the living tradition of the Christian community, we have today and we have always had different perspectives on what is meant by Christian life. But certain elements are clear. The characteristic message of Jesus was that the Reign of God was at hand, that it was accessible now and that he offered himself—his life, and eventually his death—as the pledge that it was accessible now.

The connection in the teaching of Jesus, between God's rule or reign as taken upon themselves by individuals and the publicly manifest glorious Kingdom of God, we have to learn from his parables, his commentary on the Law, and his life and death. The parables all suggest slow, quiet, hidden growth. Some suggest conflict and persecution. Jesus' commentary on the Law is radical in the strict sense that it goes to the core of the Law. Matthew tells us in the Sermon on the Mount that Jesus said, "Treat others the way you would have them treat you: this sums up the law and the prophets." (Mt. 7.12) If all of us did just that, the world would be totally transformed, society would be reshaped, and the future would explode into new possibilities. Lest anyone should think that this did not apply to gentiles, or Samaritans or Communists or people of another race or interest group or political party, the Sermon on the Mount is quite specific about this, "You have heard the commandment, 'You shall love your countryman but hate your enemy.' My command is: Love your enemies, pray for your persecutors. . . ." (Mt. 5.43-44) The heavenly Father pours out his gifts of sun and rain on all. He loves first, not measuring His love by men's merit, but loving creatively to make the response possible. It is the command of Jesus to his followers that they become perfect with that perfection of the heavenly Father to love first and love creatively, making the response possible.

In pursuit of this kind of freedom to love, Jesus counseled a quite radical detachment. His followers should not seek recognition for their good deeds and charitable contributions; they should pray in secret, should not accumulate wealth, should do the best they can without judging others, should not go to law to protect their rights, should not return injury for injury, should give cheerfully to beggars and borrowers.

Obviously, if everyone lived like this, it would be a different world. If even a significant number of people lived like this, the structures of the world would change radically. The values and principles by which the world operates are exactly the opposite of those proposed. In the structures of the world as we know it, individuals and groups accumulate as much wealth as they can and base their security upon it; they are constantly alert to protect their rights, to judge others, punish aggressors and screen out "undeserving" beggars and borrowers (which usually means those who cannot meet commercial credit qualifications). When the followers of the Baptist are wondering whether Jesus is the promised one or whether they must wait longer, Jesus points to his compassion for the poor, the oppressed and the suffering as the sign that the Kingdom of God is at hand. (Mt. 11.2-6)

The Apostles interpreted the life and death of Jesus as a fulfillment of his preaching—a life and a death of selfless compassion, of creative first loving, of utter concern that the truth of God's overwhelming mercy for mankind be made clear and of utter unconcern for his personal advantage or safety. It is this that the apostolic community saw as important in their own discipleship. It appears to have been this that led them to see the death of Jesus as the liberation of mankind. That there should be a man who was able to love first and creatively like this was the beginning of hope and an ever new beginning of trust. That someone should so love as to lay down his life not just for his friends but for those who, in effect, were his enemies was a shattering revelation of God and of what man is, and can be, in response to God.

As Christian tradition developed, we were in the habit of saying that Jesus died in obedience to the will of the Father, to atone for sin, That is, of course, correct Christian doctrine, but it must also be properly understood. It does not mean that the Father planned to have Jesus die by torture in the dawn of his manhood to appease himself for all the sins that had been committed. Such a God would be unthinkable. He would also be the very antithesis of the God Jesus preached. It does mean that the entire existence of Jesus was an expression of what God is to man—pure gift, and pure exigence, creative love—and that he would not change this even though men panicked when confronted with him and finally put him to death to get him out of the way.

In the light of the resurrection experience in which they participated, the reassembled followers of Jesus drew all these things together in their memory, and reflected upon them and gasped, asking themselves, Who was this? But this question among the followers of Jesus was different from the question as to who he was, from outsiders. For his followers the question arose because they knew exactly who he was in terms of an ordinary human and social identification.

They could speak only out of a sense of deep wonder and out of the realization of how profoundly they and the world had been transformed by the event of Jesus. And they said that this surely was uniquely God's Son, promised from all ages, Lord of all lords in history, alone able to turn over the lordship to God. They said he had ascended into the very heaven of God, to reign beside the Father judging the worth of human lives. They called Jesus the Word or utterance of God himself, the pattern of creation, born of the Father before all ages.

They knew that in Jesus the salvation of man had become self-evident, not depending on the citing of texts and authorities, that in him the face of God was clearly seen. So Christians spoke in praise of Jesus, calling him God of God, Light of Light, true God of true God, of the same reality as the Father. In Jesus Christ we have seen the face of God and have not been deceived.

NOTES

The material of this chapter is drawn largely from *God's Rule and Kingdom* by Rudolf Schnackenburg (Herder and Herder, 1963).

A very inspirational theological presentation of Jesus Christ is available in the second part of *The Christ* by Piet Schoonenborg (Herder and Herder, 1971).

An understanding of the message of Jesus should really be derived from personal reading of and meditation on the New Testament and not from anyone else's synthesis, no matter how scholarly or exhaustive.

CHAPTER VI—THE BREATH OF GOD
IN THE FOLLOWERS OF JESUS

The third section of the creeds gives us an almost breathless recital of the further content of Christian faith. In the Apostles' Creed we confess our faith in the Holy Spirit, the holy and universal Church or assembly, the sharing of the holy, the forgiveness of sins, the resurrection of the body and life everlasting. Unlike the second part of the creed, which expresses the believer's understanding or interpretation of past events, this section gives an interpretation of the present in which we live. It interprets the present as moving towards a promised future.

In the Nicene Creed this section becomes far more explicit, for we confess our faith in the Holy Spirit, the Lord and giver of life, who comes from the Father and the Son and is worshipped and glorified together with the Father and the Son, and who spoke through the prophets. We also confess faith in one holy, universal and apostolic Church and in one baptism for the forgiveness of sins, and we declare that we await the resurrection of the dead and the life of the world to come.

It may seem as though these assertions are added so hastily because they are not really important but are put there simply to complete the picture. This is not so at all. In some sense the third section is the most important section of the creeds, because it makes the whole profession of faith practically relevant to our lives in the present, as will be shown. It has three parts. It speaks of God in our own experience. Then it speaks of the community in which that experience takes place. Finally it points to the fulfillment that is to be the outcome of our striving and which has already been discussed in Chapter 2.

We have said in the earlier sections of the creeds that we put our faith in God who is hidden, who is never directly experienced, who works mysteriously in history among all men, who is to be discerned everywhere and at all times, if we cultivate the attitude of reverence and expectancy. For us, as Christians, it is in the event of Jesus Christ that God's presence in history has become concrete. This is where we know with confidence that God has acted, and this is where we know we can learn what God is like, what God asks of us, what God promises us. This is where we can be sure that we are not deceived about human hope, for we have in anticipation all that mankind can become and is called to become. This is where we know we are not talking about a fairy tale or simply expressing some wishful thinking. Here the redemption and salvation of mankind have begun very concretely, so that it becomes a rallying point, a beginning of trust, a center of creative and redemptive love, capable of radiating out to all mankind.

Nevertheless, this would help us little and would be of purely academic interest, unless this center were in fact radiating new possibilities into the world even to our own day. That God's presence was concrete and tangible in the world once long ago is not of practical interest unless it makes a difference now. It is not helpful that Jesus provides a concrete point of reference in history to help us know what God is like, what God asks of us, what God promises us, *unless* we have access to that point of reference.

One might casually suppose that the Scriptures have left us the record of the sayings and doings and sufferings of Jesus, and that each believer must make contact with Jesus and become his follower simply by the meditative reading of the Scriptures. Some Protestants, in effect, say just that. Yet anyone who has really tried to live his life by the guidance of the

Scriptures must be aware that they by no means answer all his questions, even his most important ones about life in the world today, what is right in public affairs and social issues, how to live within a professional field, and many others. We also know that very little of the life of Jesus was ever recorded and the Apostles themselves tell us that they recorded in writing very little of his teachings.

Some people hope for a clearer understanding of the Gospel from better and more extensive biblical scholarship. Yet anyone who has tried to consult reputable biblical commentaries to find inspiration and guidance in reading the meaning of the gospel in his own life will testify that he has found very meager fare indeed. They contain much technical information and yet seem to offer so little inspiration for a Christian life. In other words, the interpretation of Scripture that scholarship makes possible seems always to fall short of the questions that are important to answer in order to live as a follower of Jesus, collaborating in the redemption of the world.

This is not accidental nor is it due to personal inadequacy on the part of the biblical scholars. The interpretation that we need and are looking for is not concerned with a logical unfolding of what is there in the text; it is rather the interpretation that attempts to project what Jesus would do if he were in an entirely different situation, what the followers of Jesus should do in entirely different situations to be true to his teaching in matters that did not arise in his time at all. Moreover, it is not enough to discern what the Christian course of action might be, for we also need the conviction, hope, motivation, courage, and wisdom to carry it out and this is a matter of more than knowledge. The text of Scripture in itself could scarcely be expected to offer this kind of support.

What we claim in the creeds is that Jesus has given us not only memories of himself but that he has breathed his own spirit into us, that we might live his life creatively in his spirit, going far beyond slavish imitation of the recorded letter of his example to live by the spirit that was the key to his own life. The Apostles realized from the beginning that the spirit by which Jesus lived was that of a very devout and dedicated man. They came to see that it was the spirit of a great prophet and teacher of the ways of God. They even began to glimpse that the spirit of Jesus was the spirit of the end-time, that is, of the reign of God among men. In other words it was the spirit of the great messianic figure that would bring the final redemption of mankind from the consequences of evil deeds and would return the kingdom to the Father so that all men would find peace and fulfillment.

Looking over the life and death of Jesus in retrospect and in the light of their experience of his Resurrection, the disciples found it all coming to a clearer focus and began to see that the spirit by which Jesus lived was the very breath of God himself. They recalled that, in Israel's account of the beginning, God breathed his own breath into man and he became a living spirit. That breath of God that hovered over the waters of chaos, bringing light and life and hope to the earth, had entered in a very special way into mankind so that men were made in the very likeness of God.

And yet that likeness so constantly failed to be realized. In the covenant of Noah, the vocation of Abraham, in the Exodus and Sinai of Israel, in every prophet who listened to the call of God and proclaimed it with courage, the breath of God came again like a rushing wind, to take possession of those who would receive the abundance of life that God poured out for them. But the fullness of the Spirit, that is, of the breath of the living God could not be given because there was not a man so totally in the image and likeness of God that his own spirit could with perfect simplicity engage with and live by the Spirit of God. In retrospect, the Apostles realized, however, that Jesus was such a man, uniquely the image and Son of God, living without reservation by the breath or spirit of God, so that he was the prototype or pattern in whom all things were made, the new creation in whom the world could be redeemed.

The Apostles knew that Jesus lived by the Spirit of God and in Jesus that Spirit was revealed to them in a most intimate way as pure creative and redemptive love. It was a love not restricted to rewarding good and punishing evil, but entirely concerned with summoning the evil to turn into good and the good to become better. It was a love that laid claim to men with unhurried pace and with relentless exigence, never overwhelming or compelling men's choices with force or fear but never ceasing to challenge the conscience of men. This was the spirit of Jesus which was the Spirit of God.

The followers of Jesus also knew that it was to their community or gathering that the Spirit of Jesus had been entrusted, that they were to be his risen body in which the Spirit of God could breathe and speak to the world, summoning men to become what they are not yet and to rise to the redemptive actions that seem impossible or foolish. They realized that, up to the death of Jesus, his Spirit had not really come upon them taking possession of them. John, in his account of the conversation on the eve of Jesus' death, tells us that Jesus said of his death, "If I fail to go, the Paraclete (the Spirit) will never come to you." (Jo. 16.7) It was in dying that Jesus breathed forth his Spirit into his followers, but on condition that they would receive the Spirit by becoming themselves a community of creative and redemptive love. (Jo. 14.15-16) It was not a gift that Jesus could give to his followers singly. It was to the community that must gather that he entrusted the continued living of his life in the world, and he assures them that, although they do not now remember or understand all his teachings, the Spirit will cause them to remember and understand. (Jo. 14.26) They will know how to discern the truth of redemption and will recognize the Spirit, because that Spirit will be within them.

This is not intended only for the Apostolic age. It is the gift that we claim for the Church in all ages, pouring itself out wherever the followers of Jesus assemble in his name, trying to become a community of creative and redemptive love among themselves and towards others. We claim that we know God not only indirectly through his works in creation and history, not only by hearsay through the community's recollection of Jesus Christ as earlier generations had experience of him long ago. We claim that we know God because the breath of God really breathes within and among us, because God has become for us an intimate experience of our own lives, transforming us and bringing us to immediate participation in God's self-revelation.

For the early Church it was important to find words that properly expressed the reality the community was talking about, but it was not a matter of concern to prove the reality itself because this was evident to all who came into contact with the community of the followers of Jesus. In our times it is not so apparent. The Church has a large membership, often largely quite passive Church attenders for whom religious commitment embraces devotional activities and certain spheres of morality, but of whom it could not readily be said that the Spirit had come upon them like a mighty rushing of wind, radically changing their perception of everything so that they must be either drunk or seized with the gift of prophecy. Moreover, for many people the Church's elaborate worldwide organization and governmental structure quite obscures its character of community of charity living by the Spirit of God, testifying to the truth of redemption so as to bring unity and hope to all mankind.

Meanwhile, however, although the Church looks so much like a great cultural tradition that its members take for granted, our whole way of life is a constant invitation to a radical conversion in the Spirit. Every time we baptize someone, we give him the commitment of the community that it will draw him into the circle of its creative love, lifting him above the network of sin in the world and giving him opportunities to live by the light of the Risen Christ and in the Spirit. If the person being baptized is an adult, we ask of him a complementary commitment to live in the community, sharing its task of redemption. If he is a small child, we extend an invitation to him which we hope he will accept when he is mature for such decisions.

Every time we confirm someone, we are praying that the Spirit may come upon him so that he will actively participate in the Church, that is, in building it up as a community of creative and redemptive love, and in sharing its mission to testify to the world. At this stage the candidate should be ready to make his personal commitment to active membership and should have shown signs of openness to the Spirit. At present we often find that people were confirmed when they were so young that they were not ready for any personal commitment and in fact presented themselves for the sacrament simply because they were expected to do so along with everyone in their age group, as in the initiation rites of traditional cultures.

It is probably for this reason that the Pentecostal Movement became so popular so rapidly among Catholics of our times. In it they experience what they have missed at their confirmation; they find an opportunity to make a personal commitment publicly within a community of personally committed people, where the presence of the Spirit is evident and is explicitly sought and valued as the basis for the life of the Church.

When we refer to the Spirit in the pattern of our creeds, we shape them into a trinitarian pattern. We declare our faith in the Father, the Son and the Holy Spirit. In each case we are speaking of the One God. By putting it this way we are really insisting on a paradox that we cannot and will not resolve. We know and acknowledge the transcendent God of Israel, and with Israel we confess that God is one and that there can be no other gods beside him, because any other god could only be a false god or idol, or, in effect, no god at all.

At the same time we profess that in Jesus we have met God himself. In the face of Jesus we have seen the face of God. The presence of Jesus is the presence of God. But God remains transcendent and Jesus himself prays to the Father. It is important to us to maintain that in Jesus we have met God, because if God is not as we have seen him revealed in Jesus Christ, then all our hope is based on false premises. We are confident that what we have seen God to be like in Jesus Christ is what he really is.

Similarly, we claim that by the Spirit that is in us we have true knowledge of God and that we are not deceived. We assert that by the Spirit that lives in the community of the followers of Jesus, God reveals himself to us immediately. We are confident that we can trust that revelation and participate in it without fear of betrayal or ultimate confusion. We are convinced that God really is as he has shown himself to us in our history and experience.

This is what Christians mean when they speak of God as Triune, saying that we have encountered God as Father, as Son and as Holy Spirit, but these three are one God. It is not a statement that appeals to philosophers, and philosophical explanations of what we mean always make it all so abstract and remote that it becomes an irrelevant doctrine. It is simply a faithful statement of our Christian experience in the community of believers through the ages, and we will stand by it whether or not philosophers can explain it, because it is our experience.

NOTES

A good collection of essays on the Spirit is available in *God, Jesus, Spirit* edited by Daniel Callahan (Herder and Herder, 1970).

The explanation here given of the doctrine of the Trinity is summarized from that of Josef Ratzinger in *Introduction to Christianity* (Herder and Herder, 1971).

CHAPTER VII—FELLOWSHIP AND RECONCILIATION

In the creeds we confess our faith in the universal Church, the sharing of the holy and the forgiveness of sins, further elaborated as one, holy, universal and apostolic Church and one baptism for the remission of sins. Most people realize that the expression, Catholic, is so old in this context, that it has no reference to the schisms in the Church between Catholic and Protestant or even between Catholic and Orthodox, but has reference simply to the one and universal Church. It may be less obvious that the idea of one, holy catholic and apostolic Church is really an eschatological one. It is like the vision in the book of Revelation of the new Jerusalem, the holy city, coming down out of heaven from God. (Rev. 21.2) We profess our faith in it, not because we have noticed that it already exists, but because it is what we are striving to bring about.

The New Testament word for Church means assembly, and what we are concerned with is not so much a ready-made assembly, fully constituted from the beginning, but rather a long process of assembling or gathering the church that is to be from the four corners of the earth and from all nations. In terms of that final assembly of the people of God that is truly one, truly holy, truly universal and truly apostolic, every Church institution and every gathering and union is still relative. In one of our oldest Eucharistic prayers, preserved in the document we know as the *Didache*, we ask that, just as the bread we break is one loaf made of many grains once scattered about the hillsides, so the assembly of the Lord may be gathered into one into the Kingdom of God.

When we profess faith in one, holy, catholic and apostolic Church, we pledge ourselves to become such a church, true to the apostolic legacy and intent, universal in its concern and in its creative love, holy with the holiness of Jesus and the Spirit which is the single-heartedness of creative and redemptive love, and genuinely one in this endeavor. Such a profession of faith is anything but a casual remark for it implies readiness to collaborate in the redemption with all who are willing to work towards it. It also implies an attitude of service to others. Membership is not passive, as though the Church were the assembly of the redeemed or saved, and the main concern were with membership as such. The Church as we have it from the Apostles implies that membership is always intended to be active, that is, concerned with the redemption of the world, of others even outside the institutional church memberships. It implies that membership of the Church is a vocation on behalf of others, a vocation to help in a special way to discern and to foster whatever is for the unity and hope of all mankind.

The Church in history tries to bring about the gathering of the great assembly of the end-time or final reign of God, primarily by what she is—the presence in history of the fulfillment that is yet to come, the anticipation in germ or nucleus of what is to be for all. The Church tries to be what Jesus asked us to be—the extension of his presence in the world, by making ourselves a community of creative and redemptive love bringing about the new creation, offering genuinely new possibilities to the world and the men within it, beginning with those within the community itself.

This is why the one really basic structure of the Church is Eucharist, the celebration of the death of the Lord until he comes. Eucharist is the means that Jesus himself gave to his followers to assemble into a church. They tell us that the night before he suffered he spoke with them at great length, knowing that they still did not really understand either his message or his life and that they were therefore ill-equipped to understand his death or to come to see how his death could possibly be redemption for mankind. They then record that he carefully set his own death within the context of the Passover *seder* celebration. In that celebration, the households of Israel recall the mercies of God who liberated them from Egypt precisely through their terrible sufferings there, so that in the unleavened bread of their affliction they were able to respond to God's call to the radically new, uncontaminated with the leavening from the old, soured dough .

Jesus took that bread into his hands, knowing that, for his disciples as for him, the Passover bread was already rich with many accumulated layers of meaning and connotation. As he broke it, he spoke to them in prophetic style they would have recognized, and said, "This is my body which shall be given for you." And over the wine he said, "This is the cup of the renewal of covenant and it is my blood which shall be shed for you." Then he invited them to celebrate this action after his death, each time trying to understand his death within the context of Exodus, understand his death as the new Exodus through which God would liberate and fashion himself a great people. The celebration of this mystery was to be for his followers the tent of meeting, the place of assembling. In their effort to understand and respond with their own commitment, they were to become one people with one purpose.

The explanatory phrase in the Apostles' Creed, "the sharing of the holy," which we usually translate "the communion of saints," seems to have been intended as a discreet reference to the Eucharistic assembly and celebration, by which the Church is essentially constituted. There is some doubt that it is correctly translated "communion of saints," because early references are clearly concerned with the sharing of "holy things" rather than of holy persons. This referred to "the mysteries," that is, the sacramental celebrations themselves, which are thought of as giving access to the world beyond, the world yet to come, the world of the resurrection and the fulfillment, already mysteriously anticipated by the community's sharing in the experience of the Resurrection of Christ. Later the phrase was taken as meaning the sharing with the holy ones, that is, with those who had already passed on into the life of the world to come and were victorious and blessed with Christ. But that sharing happens precisely through the celebration of the Eucharist.

When, therefore, we assert this communion or sharing, we express our interpretation of the reality that takes place in the celebration of the Eucharist and in the ongoing life of the Church. Again, it is an interpretation that demands action. It demands that the Eucharist be, so to speak, the peak or summit of a Christian life in the sense that all effort and all life contributes to it and that all effort and all life flows from it, transformed. The testimony that we have from the early Church makes it clear that that transformation of the lives of the sharers of the Eucharist was expected to be accessible to experience. The charity of Christ and the indwelling of the Holy Spirit were expected to be visible in their fruits, that is, in attitudes and actions by which a community of charity was really built up and constantly extended to newcomers.

The other explanatory phrase, "the forgiveness of

sins," refers not to the sacrament of Penance as we have it today, but as the Nicene Creed further specifies, to the "one baptism for the remission of sins." The one baptism is the entering into the death of Jesus in order to be reborn out of the waters of chaos into the new creation which is the anticipation of the world yet to come in the Resurrection of Jesus. The community asserts without hesitation that it is only in the cross of Jesus that there is reconciliation and forgiveness of sins and new freedom from the accumulated consequences of evil deeds.

The sins from which we are guaranteed remission, forgiveness or reconciliation in the creeds are not only particular personal sins that an individual might have committed before his baptism if he is an adult, but include the sins and consequences of sins that constitute the state of sin or unredemption and unfreedom in the world. By passing through the experience of the death of Christ, the community hopes that in the terrible affliction it can leave behind the contaminating effects of the old and step into the totally new world of the Resurrection. It knows that the way to do this is to receive the Spirit of Jesus in its midst and live together as a community in the continuance of the creative and redemptive love that brought Jesus to his death and made of his death the great Exodus or crossing over the bounds of the possible.

The baptism refers to community as a whole and also to its new members who are instructed as to the meaning and experiences of this community before their arrival and are then allowed a ritual participation in the constitutive events in the history of the community. By this they are encouraged toward a very practical understanding of what adoption into and membership in the community mean for them and

This reconciliation and remission of sins cannot be a reality in the sacramental context of the initiation of new members and the celebration of the Eucharist, if it is not the style of life of the community as a whole. The Church at all levels and in all its manifestations is intended to be a community of fellowship and reconciliation, in which redemptive and reconciling initiatives become possible, that would be impossible otherwise. This is the mission of the Church that we all have directly from Jesus Christ himself. It does not require any mandate from hierarchic sources and it does not depend on Church institutions, ecclesiastical approval, or complex organization. Yet it is the very stuff and substance of the life of the Church.

The goals of fellowship and reconciliation can not be limited to the Church membership in the institutional Churches. The community of the followers of Jesus is intended to work as a leaven in the world, making fellowship and reconciliation more possible at all levels of society and in all spheres of life, including its political and economic aspects. We open up new possibilities for others by realizing them in our own lives. And we are confident that we can do that because we have a vision of the end-time in the person of Jesus Christ and because we strive to realize that vision in the power of the Spirit, already tasting in some sense, through the community of charity, the resurrection of the dead and the life of the world yet to come.

NOTES

The understanding of Church here presented is drawn largely from the documents of Vatican II, mainly *Lumen Gentium* (the Constitution on the Church) and *Sacrosanctum Concilium* (the Constitution on the Liturgy).

There is a difficult but very rewarding essay on this topic entitled "The Church and Mankind" by Edward Schillebeeckx, O.P., in the first volume of the *Concilium* series (Paulist Press, 1965). Any of the writings of Karl Rahner on the topic of Church and sacraments are to be strongly recommended, though the vocabulary might be too specialized for many readers.

The particular sacraments have been touched very lightly in this and the previous chapter because they have been discussed in my earlier book, *The Meaning of the Sacraments* (Pflaum Press, 1972).

CONCLUSION—CONFESSION OF FAITH

We believe that happiness awaits mankind and that our existence is not absurd.

We believe that all men's longings can be fulfilled beyond imagining and that hope is not in vain.

We believe that we come into existence by love and that our lives can become wholly meaningful by love.

We believe that all men are joined in one destiny and that we are all responsible for one another.

We believe that peace, justice and freedom from want are God's gift to all men but that they must be freely received by mankind.

We believe that no human being is forgotten by God and that no one can be unimportant to us.

We believe it because of Jesus who has reflected to us the fidelity of the Father.

We believe it because of the sublime simplicity of his preaching and of his life.

We believe it because of the luminous conviction and singleness of purpose with which he faced death.

We believe it because the Father has raised him up as a sign of hope and challenge to all mankind that shall one day be gloriously fulfilled.

We believe it because of the Spirit that is among the followers of Jesus to this day.

We believe it because of the assembling of the nations in unity and hope that has been begun and must yet be completed.

We believe it because we share in the celebration of the mysteries in which we are transformed.

We believe it because we expect to share in the fulfillment of all the promises in a world yet to come.

Let it be so: this is our commitment.